COMPLETE CRAP

COMPLETE CRAP

Michael Powell

Michael O'Mara Humour

First published in Great Britain in 2002 by
Michael O'Mara Books Limited
9 Lion Yard
Tremadoc Road
London SW4 7NQ

The material in this compilation first appeared in *The Little Book of Crap Excuses* and *The Little Book of Crap Advice* by Michael Powell copyright © 2001 Michael Powell, published by Michael O'Mara Books Ltd.

A CIP catalogue record for this book is available from the British Library

ISBN 1-85479-313-6

1 3 5 7 9 10 8 6 4 2

Designed and typeset by Design 23

Printed and bound by Bookmarque Limited UK

CRAP
EXCUSES

RULES FOR MAKING EXCUSES

Just because an excuse is rubbish doesn't mean you shouldn't use it.

Always base an excuse on the truth, unless you are a very good liar.

A good excuse saves a load of explanation.

You're never too old to learn a new excuse.

A bad excuse is better than nothing.

The better the excuse, the sooner it's over.

All excuses come to those who are late.

There is a time to speak and a time to make excuses.

Always put off today what you can excuse tomorrow.

One good excuse deserves another.

An excuse is its own reward.

Many excuses make light work.

No excuse like the first excuse.

A man without an excuse is but half
a man.

NEE NAW NEE NAW

**Just pull over to the side of the road,
sir...**

I didn't know I was speeding. I must
have nodded off.

I usually go much faster than this and
I've never been stopped before.

Your headlights were blinding me. I was
trying to get away.

My speedometer just broke.

My wife left me last week for a police officer, and I thought you were him trying to give her back!

I was speeding to waste petrol.

I wanted to send a message to OPEC that this country won't be held to ransom by rising oil prices.

I claim political asylum.

Why were you going that fast?

Have you ever tried to drive a car like this below eighty?

But my dog was driving!

I'm in a hurry, officer. Your wife is expecting me.

Yeah. I was speeding towards you. You looked like you could use some help.

The Earth is travelling round the sun at over a hundred thousand miles per hour: what's an extra thirty?

I was getting a bag of crack cocaine out of the glove compartment when my gun fell off my lap and got jammed between the brake and accelerator pedals.

I lost my hamster this morning and I was hoping you would give me a full cavity search.

I thought it was OK to go ten over the speed limit.

THE FATHER OF ALL EXCUSES?

This is a confession a friend sent me – I would certainly never try this!

A couple of years ago in South Africa we attended a party one Saturday night. I'd had a few drinks already when a friend came running to me with my youngest son in his arms. The four-year-old had been found drinking a bottle of whisky. My wife and I had to rush him to hospital to get his stomach pumped.

As I sped to hospital I drove into a police roadblock where they tested for drunk driving. I knew I was in trouble and didn't even bother to explain. I blew into their apparatus and it proved me legally drunk.

I told the policeman that I didn't drink and that his apparatus must be faulty. He gave me another apparatus to blow in and I told my youngest to blow in the pipe. He also registered as being legally drunk. The policeman couldn't believe his eyes and let us go without further questions.

IMPOTENCE

It doesn't matter, I'm happy just to cuddle...

This is the first time this has happened to me today.

I guess it's just nature's way of saying 'no hard feelings'.

I'm suffering from Ascension Deficit Disorder.

I knew I shouldn't have given blood today.

I'm sorry, it seems to be set for Hillary, not Monica.

I guess my pointer just turned into a setter.

I'm turgidly challenged.

I'm saving myself for the match tomorrow.

I just spilled a bottle of fabric conditioner down my trousers.

I'm sorry, I can't imagine anyone I like right now.

IT'S MORE THAN MY JOB'S WORTH...

We don't know how to do that.

It's too late to do that today. Come back tomorrow after 5 p.m.

The person who deals with that is on sabbatical.

It isn't cost effective.

I'm new.

I'm new.
(Said by the same person seven months later.)

I'm not authorized to tell you.

Our computer system is:
> down/
> being replaced/
> being delivered tomorrow.

You've reached the wrong department.

We've lost your file – you don't exist.

It's Tuesday.

IT'S A FAIR COP...

Dumb criminal excuses

Two teenage joyriders in Florida were bailed after stealing their twenty-fifth car in two years. When they left the courthouse they immediately stole number twenty-six and crashed it less than an hour later. Their excuse was that they didn't have enough money for the bus fare home.

A death row inmate in Siberia strangled his cellmate, cut out his liver and boiled it in a metal mug. His excuse was that he wanted to avoid execution by pretending to be insane.

In Union, Kentucky, in 1993, two burglars were arrested after a failed house robbery. After they had ransacked the house, their car wouldn't start. So they went back inside and pleaded with the owner not to call the police. They even offered to put the stolen goods back and tidy up. Then they tried unsuccessfully to start their car a second time and asked the owner for a jump-start. When the police arrived, their excuse for the robbery was to get money to fix their car.

A Frenchman arrested for shooting his wife blamed a TV strike. 'There was nothing to look at. I was bored,' he said.

In 1987, an Australian was arrested for kicking his mother to death. His excuse: he had been listening to Bob Dylan's music.

In 1992, a sixteen-year-old boy was arrested for armed robbery of a jewellery store. His excuse: to get money to pay off his overdue library books.

A NOTE FROM YOUR MOTHER...

A list of real excuses written by parents on their children's sick notes

Please excuse James from being absent on June 28, 29, 30, 31, 32 and also 33.

Please excuse Robbie from being. It was his father's fault.

Please excuse Jane. She is having trouble with her ovals.

Richard has been away because he has had two teeth taken off his face.

My son is under the doctor and should not take fizical ed. Please execute him.

Please excuse Joanna from being at school yesterday. She was in bed with gramps.

Please excuse Roland from P.E. for a few days. Yesterday he fell out of a tree and misplaced his hip.

Lee was absent yesterday because he was playing football. He was hit in his growing part.

Alison won't be at school a week from Monday. We have to go to her funeral.

I kept Rachel home because she had to go Christmas shopping because I don't know what size she wear.

My daughter was absent yesterday because she spent the weekend with the Marines and was exhausted.

Please excuse Eloise for being absent. She was sick and I had her shot.

Please excuse Veronica from Jim today. She is administrating.

Victoria could not come to school today because she has been bothered by very close veins.

Andrew will not be in school cus he has an acre in his side.

Please excuse Roy from school. He has very loose vowels.

Please excuse Fred for being absent yesterday. He had diarrhoea and his boots leak.

Louis was absent yesterday because he missed his bust.

Please excuse Annabel for missing school yesterday. We forgot to get the Sunday paper off the doormat, and when we found it on Monday, we thought it was Sunday.

Please excuse Jamie for being absent yesterday. He had a cold and could not breed well.

Olivia was absent yesterday as she was having a gangover.

Maryann was absent for five days because she had a fever, sore throat, headache and upset stomach. Her sister was also sick, fever and sore throat, her brother had a low grade fever and ached all over. I wasn't the best either, sore throat and fever. There must be something going around, her father even got hot last night.

List attributed to Nisheeth Parekh, University of Texas Medical Branch, Galveston

EAT, THEN CHEAT

If you eat something in secret, it has no calories.

If you have a diet drink with any other food, the calories are cancelled out by the diet drink.

When you are eating with someone else, if they eat more than you do then your calories don't count.

Food used for medicinal reasons doesn't count, such as brandy, honey, ice cream and chocolate cake.

Food licked off knives and spoons when

cooking has no calories.

When you eat food at the cinema, the calories don't count because they are part of the entertainment.

Food has to have calories to be fattening.

Calories are a measure of heat, so eating frozen food, like ice cream, will actually make you lose weight.

Any food eaten after you have just weighed yourself doesn't count.

SAVE POUNDS!!

Use cheap scales because they always weigh half a stone lighter.

Never weigh with wet hair.

Go to the toilet first.

Take all your clothes off; remove glasses, body jewellery, make up and prosthetics; cut your nails, squeeze your spots, cut your hair, shave your legs and clean your ears.

Raise your hands above your head to make you lighter.

Breathe out!

DOCTOR, DOCTOR!

On 7 September 1999, a doctor in America ended a successful Caesarean section with a bizarre act that landed him with a five million-dollar lawsuit and the nickname 'Dr Zorro'. Witnesses in the operating theatre allege that he carved his initials, 'A' and 'Z' on the woman's stomach in letters three inches high. He is said to have excused himself at the time with the words: 'I did such a beautiful job, I'll initial it.' The doctor's licence has been suspended.

KINKY

When, in December 1996, a thirty-two-year-old man from Kentucky shot himself in the left shoulder with a .22-calibre rifle, he told paramedics it was 'to see how it felt'.

He did the same again a year later because it 'felt so good' the last time, he just had to do it again.

IT JUST CAME OUT OF NOWHERE ...

Real car insurance claims

The other vehicle collided with mine without giving any warning of its intentions.

I started to slow down but the traffic was more stationary than I thought.

My car was legally parked as it backed into the other car.

The old man was all over the road.
I had to swerve several times before
I hit him.

Trying to kill a fly, I drove into a
telegraph pole.

I thought my window was down, but
realized it wasn't when my head went
through it.

Returning home, I drove into the wrong
house and hit a tree I haven't got.

I had been driving for forty years when
I fell asleep at the wheel and crashed
the car.

I was going at about 70 or 80 m.p.h.
when my girlfriend on the pillion
reached over and grabbed my testicles
so I lost control.

The indirect cause of the accident was a
little man in a small car with a big
mouth.

I moved away from the kerb, looked at my mother-in-law and drove over the embankment.

To avoid hitting the car in front, I struck the pedestrian.

TOP TEN EXCUSES TO USE WHEN PRESENTING YOURSELF AT A HOSPITAL WITH A VEGETABLE LODGED UP YOUR BACKSIDE

I was just cleaning some vegetables in the shower when . . .

I was just digging on my allotment when there was a solar eclipse . . .

I was walking past the vegetable section in the supermarket when I slipped and . . .

I was attacked in the park by an 8-foot rabbit. He did some bad things, doctor.

My teeth hurt so I haven't been chewing my food properly for a while now.

I'm very absent-minded. I meant to put it in the fridge.

There was this chutney recipe. I was just following the instructions.

My dog . . .

I was kidnapped by aliens. They took me up to their mother ship and did lots of tests. My memory is very hazy. I think you'd better take a look . . .

I was sunbathing naked in the garden when a bunch of kids started throwing vegetables over the fence.

FIVE EXCUSES TO USE WHEN PRESENTING YOURSELF AT A HOSPITAL WITH A WINE BOTTLE LODGED UP YOUR BACKSIDE

I was just opening a bottle of wine in the shower when . . .

I lost my corkscrew.

I practise tantric meditation and I was trying out a new posture.

I was the guest of honour at the launch of an ocean liner. Well, the Dom Perignon sort of glanced off the hull and . . .

A mate told me that you can't beat the feeling of sticking a bottle up your arse.

SO EMBARRASSING IT HAS TO BE TRUE ...

A colleague called in one Monday morning to report that he wouldn't be in that day. Apparently he'd accompanied his girlfriend – for moral support you understand – while she had her tongue pierced. Obviously the girlfriend was made of sterner stuff than my colleague, so when the talk turned to the piercing of other body parts our hero began to feel a little faint, and went outside to take a few deep breaths.

Unfortunately, his squeamishness got the better of him and he passed out cold on the pavement. He ended up being taken to casualty by his girlfriend – for moral support you understand – to have six staples put in the back of his head.

We're convinced he was fit to work on the Monday, but was too embarrassed...

YOU'VE NEVER HAD IT SO GOOD

Politicians' excuses and lies – what they really mean...

•

WE HAVE NO QUARREL WITH THEIR PEOPLE...
We will bomb the suckers until the crazy guy with the moustache has no one left to rule.

•

WE HAVE NO ALTERNATIVE BUT TO USE FORCE.
Let's try out these new smart bombs.

•

COLLATERAL DAMAGE WAS KEPT TO A MINIMUM.
The Chinese embassy was just too shiny to ignore.

•

WE MUST NOT INTERFERE IN THIS
DELICATE MATTER.
This country doesn't produce any oil.

•

THIS COUNTRY WILL NOT BE HELD
TO RANSOM BY PUBLIC OPINION.
Democracy sucks.

•

IT IS NOT IN THE PUBLIC INTEREST.
If anyone finds out, we're screwed.

•

THERE IS NO RISK TO PUBLIC
HEALTH.
See you next year. I'll be in my bunker.

•

IT WAS AN ERROR OF JUDGEMENT.
...and if it wasn't for you pesky kids I'd
never have been caught. Can I have my
job back now?

•

TALKS WERE SUBSTANTIVE.
OK, we've agreed on deep crust
pepperoni, but the chicken wings are
non-negotiable.

•

THAT IS NOT FOR ME TO SAY.
I haven't been briefed on this bit.

•

IT IS EVERY CITIZEN'S RIGHT . . .
We can afford that.

•

STATISTICALLY, IT IS STILL A VERY
SAFE MEANS OF TRANSPORT.
Cancel my ticket, I'm walking.

•

IT WAS A VERY HUMBLING
EXPERIENCE.
It was squalid and depressing.

•

WITH RESPECT . . .
Do you want some or what? Don't mess
with me, asshole. I know where you live.

•

I LISTENED WITH INTEREST.
I was so bored I nearly chewed my arm off.

•

I AM NOT GOING TO PRE-EMPT THE
REPORT.
I haven't had a chance to bribe the
judge yet.

•

THERE HAS BEEN NO BREACH OF
NATIONAL SECURITY.
What do you mean they stole *all* the
passwords?

•

A WEEK IS A LONG TIME IN POLITICS.
My mind's gone blank. Say something,
quick…

•

SOMETIMES POLITICIANS HAVE TO
MAKE TOUGH DECISIONS.
If you all put your money in this bag
and lie face down on the floor, no one
will get hurt.

•

THAT'S WHY I BECAME A POLITICIAN.
...apart from the power, status, casual
sex and diplomatic immunity.

•

THAT IS FOR THE ELECTORATE TO
DECIDE.
We don't have a policy yet.

WE LISTEN TO THEIR OPINIONS.
It's a marginal seat.

•

WE TAKE THIS MATTER VERY
SERIOUSLY INDEED.
Next time, we'll make damn sure no
one finds out.

I'D LOVE TO BUT...

I have to floss my cat.

My crayons all melted together.

I don't want to leave my comfort zone.

I'm trying to cut down.

I'm still looking for my other kidney.

I have to dispose of a body.

My dog ate my contact lenses.

Someone just stapled my knees together.

BIBLICAL EXCUSES

That's a nice story, but now tell me where you've really been for the last three days.
JONAH'S MOTHER

It was a bit muddy.
WHY MOSES WAS RELUCTANT TO CROSS THE
RED SEA

You can't get the wood these days.
WHY ABRAHAM DIDN'T SACRIFICE ISAAC

She made me do it!
ADAM, ON WHY HE SPENT EVERY SATURDAY
OUT SHOPPING FOR CLOTHES AFTER BEING
CAST OUT OF THE GARDEN OF EDEN

I didn't know it was going to be so loud!
JOSHUA, AFTER THE WALLS OF JERICHO CAME
TUMBLING DOWN

I was really bored.
GOD'S EXCUSE FOR THE SEVEN PLAGUES OF
EGYPT

*Sorry about the myrrh – they didn't have
any teddy bears.*
BALTHAZAR

Dinosaurs? What dinosaurs?
NOAH

The Devil makes work for idle hands.
GOD ON THE CREATION OF WOMAN

I didn't know my own strength.
SAMSON

I'm not eating that – it's not kosher.
A LION, ON SEEING DANIEL

I didn't say kill the infants. I said kill the ants!
HEROD

He started it!
CAIN, ON ABEL

Sorry, Goliath, I didn't know it was loaded.
DAVID

I had a puncture.
THE PRODIGAL SON

EXCUSES FOR DIALLING 999

The following are real 999 calls made to the Metropolitan Police

Do you know a good stain remover?

There's a rat in my kitchen.

My bike was stolen last week.

I can't turn my tap off.

I think my neighbour is a spy.

I've found an umbrella. Where should I take it?

What time is it?

And Greater Manchester Police

Please send an officer to clear away some refuse sacks left behind by the binmen.

I've filled up my car with diesel instead of petrol. What should I do?

Could you tell me some train times please?

My road map has blown out of the car window – could you tell me where I am?

The emergency services are always extremely busy with genuine calls. Don't waste their time – engage your brain before you dial!

DID THEY REALLY THINK THESE WOULD WORK?

They said (allegedly) ...

The streets are safe in Philadelphia; it's only the people that make them unsafe.
FORMER PHILADELPHIA MAYOR AND POLICE CHIEF FRANK RIZZO

The President has kept all of the promises he intended to keep.
FORMER CLINTON AIDE GEORGE
STEPHANOPOULOS SPEAKING ON
LARRY KING LIVE

•

Without censorship, things can get terribly confused in the public mind.
GENERAL WILLIAM WESTMORELAND,
US ARMY

•

It isn't pollution that's harming the environment. It's impurities in our air and water that are doing it.
DAN QUAYLE, FORMER US VICE PRESIDENT

•

Outside of the killings, Washington has one of the lowest crime rates in the country.
FORMER MAYOR MARION BARRY,
WASHINGTON, DC

•

I haven't committed a crime. What I did was fail to comply with the law.
DAVID DINKINS, FORMER NEW YORK CITY MAYOR

•

I was under medication when I made the decision to burn the tapes.
RICHARD NIXON, FORMER US PRESIDENT

•

We are not without accomplishment. We have managed to distribute poverty equally.
NGUYEN CO THATCH, VIETNAMESE FOREIGN MINISTER

•

We don't necessarily discriminate. We simply exclude certain types of people.
COLONEL GERALD WELLMAN, ROYAL OFFICER TRAINING CORPS INSTRUCTOR

•

I've always thought that underpopulated countries in Africa are vastly under-polluted.
LAWRENCE SUMMERS, CHIEF ECONOMIST OF THE WORLD BANK, ON THE ISSUE OF EXPORTING TOXIC WASTE TO THE THIRD WORLD

●

When the President does it, that means it is not illegal.
RICHARD NIXON, FORMER US PRESIDENT

●

In any country there must be people who have to die. They are the sacrifices any nation has to make to achieve law and order.
IDI AMIN, FORMER PRESIDENT OF UGANDA

●

Sometimes democracy must be bathed in blood.
GENERAL AUGUSTO PINOCHET, FORMER PRESIDENT OF CHILE

●

*We are not retreating – we are
advancing in another direction.*
GENERAL DOUGLAS MACARTHUR, US ARMY

WE'LL SEE...

Parents to children

We didn't have them when we were
your age.

You can have/do/eat it when you're
older/taller.

If you'd just told me the truth in the first
place...

I left my wallet in another time zone.

EXCUSE FOR MISSING GEOGRAPHY LESSONS?

A woman called to make reservations at a travel agency in America.

'I want to go from Chicago to Hippopotamus, New York.'

The agent was at a loss for words. Finally, the agent said: 'Are you sure that's the name of the town?'

'Yes, what flights do you have?' replied the customer.

After some searching, the agent came back with, 'I'm sorry, ma'am, I've looked up every airport code in the country and can't find a Hippopotamus anywhere.'

The customer retorted, 'Oh don't be silly. Everyone knows where it is. Check your map!'

The agent scoured a map of the state of New York and finally offered, 'You don't mean Buffalo, do you?'

'That's it! I knew it was a big animal!'

IT WASN'T MY FAULT!

More car insurance claims

I pulled into a lay-by with smoke coming from under the bonnet. I realised the car was on fire so took my dog and smothered it with a blanket.

An invisible car appeared from nowhere, hit my car and vanished.

On the M6 I moved from the centre lane to the fast lane but the other car didn't give way.

A truck backed through my windscreen into my wife's face.

I was sure that the old man would never reach the other side of the road, when I struck him.

I had one eye on a parked car, another on approaching lorries, and another on the woman behind.

I told the police officer that I was unhurt, but upon removing my helmet discovered I had a fractured skull.

I had been shopping for plants all day and was returning home. As I reached a junction a hedge sprang up, obscuring my view, and I did not see the other vehicle.

I was driving to the doctor with rear end trouble when my universal joint gave way, causing me to crash.

On approach to the traffic lights the car in front suddenly broke.

FIT FOR LIFE? FIT FOR NOTHING...

Here are some excuses doctors and physical therapists heard from patients, explaining why they can't exercise

An earthquake drained my pool.

My dog ate my running shoes.

I can't exercise because of the grizzly bear. (Heard near a popular walking path in Anchorage, Alaska.)

My wife would be angry with me if I lost weight.

If I exercise, I might not have enough energy left over for sex.

I can't because of the volcanic ash.

The TV at the gym is always on something I don't want to watch.

THE NEXT TRAIN ON PLATFORM *CRACKLE* IS THE DELAYED *SQUAWK* TO *CCCRRRRR*... OH I GIVE UP. TAXI!!

Real excuses given to passengers for late or cancelled trains

I'm ever so sorry. We've run out of fuel.

The wrong kind of weather.

A 34 per cent increase in delays due to increasing suicides.

We are not removing the buddleia fast enough.

We have to do more.

The wrong kind of snow.

Fleas in the driver's cab.

The wrong kind of leaves.

We didn't stop at the last scheduled station because of skiddy tracks.

The service is delayed today because the driver is only five feet one and his swivel chair has broken. He's too short to reach the pedals.

The driver is still eating his sandwiches.

There was a problem with the rostering. The driver is sunning himself on the Algarve and there is no one else to drive the train.

We've got a problem with rabbits and have to keep an eye on their burrowing ... rabbit warrens have already added to the instability of cuttings and caused a landslide after a flash flood.

I apologise for the delay but the computer controlling the signalling has the Monday Morning Blues.

I STILL LOVE YOU AS A FRIEND...

Breaking up with a partner

I guess I'm just not ready to commit.

I just need some space. I'm becoming an astronaut.

I just need some time. Can you come back in twenty years?

You deserve better.

It's me, not you.

The only thing we have in common is
that we got married on the same day.

God loves me and I know he has a
better life for me without you.

I'm holding you back.

I went through a past-life regression and
it turns out that we were brother and
sister in Ancient Egypt. So we can't see
each other any more. It would be incest.

I can't see you any more. I have a
detached retina.

I respect you too much. And I'm afraid
you'd throw away all my back issues of
Hustler, if you ever found them.

I'm married to my job.

I'd love to grow old with you, but
you're too far in front for me to catch
up.

We've drifted apart. I'll stay in the boat
and you swim for help.

We're two different people. Actually, I'm three.

No, of course there's no one else. But if there was, she'd have better tits than you.

I didn't know true happiness until I met you. And then it was too late.

OF COURSE I WANT TO SEE YOU...

Missing a date

The cat exploded and I had to take it to the vet.

I don't want to ruin our friendship.

I'm not your type. I'm not inflatable.

I'm washing my hair on Friday night, so I can't see you. Saturday? Well, it's got to dry hasn't it?

I don't date outside my own species.

IS THAT THE TIME?

Ways to end a bad date

Wow. That's amazing. I like watching TV too.

How many kids shall we have?

Would you like to hear your name in Klingon?

Sorry, I'm a little preoccupied. I'm expecting a call. My wife could go into labour at any moment.

I've really matured. Last year I'd never have bothered with someone who looks like you.

I love cats, too. How do you like to cook them?

The alarm on my watch has gone off. Does that mean it's time for my medication or yours?

Most of the voices in my head really like you! It's been really nice, but I have to scream now.

Can we stop at the clinic? I need to pick up some results.

Let's get the bill. The Viagra will be wearing off soon.

I've been wanting to date you since I read about you on a toilet wall last year.

I can't wait to show you some of the sex tricks I learned in prison.

…so now I've just got one big nostril. Can I borrow your mirror?

…and so by touching your hand I am able to make a complete replica…

Boy, there's lots of skin on you. I should be able to finish that sewing project tonight.

My mission on your planet is nearing its conclusion.

My three favourite hobbies are meeting people, power tools and unblocking my drains.

I have a uterus in a jar at home. Would you like to see it?

WE WAS ROBBED...

Sport

It was like being in a foreign country.
IAN RUSH ON THE DIFFICULTY OF PLAYING ABROAD

We actually got the winner three minutes from the end but then they equalized.
IAN MCNAIL

Sure there have been injuries and deaths in boxing – but none of them serious.
ALAN MINTER

People think we make $3 million and $4 million a year. They don't realize that most of us only make $500,000.

Pete Incaviglia, baseball player

•

Golfing Goofs

I hit my stomach during the swing.

I play better when I can hit the ball.

The air is very heavy today.

That shot would have been perfect if it hadn't hit the tree.

The ball must have hit a low-pressure air pocket.

If I had some of Tiger Woods' money, I'd be able to buy a decent set of clubs, too.

It would have been a birdie if the ball hadn't stopped.

I'm wearing my sensible trousers today.

Rugby

It was a choice between his head and the ball, so I kicked the one with less hair.

He snatched the ball off me, splashing me with mud, so then I got really mad ...

•

Football Own Goals

The goalkeeper obstructed my view of the goal.

I don't play well on a Sunday.

I'm saving myself for the final.

I was too busy kicking spectators.

I don't believe in training. It destroys spontaneity.

I had a kebab half an hour ago and I still feel like I'm dragging a ten-pound turd around in my stomach.

I don't have my lucky earrings on today.

•

Weightlifting

You mean that crack cocaine cut with bull semen isn't a cure for the flu?

•

Long Jump

Whad'ya mean 'no jump'? I didn't just leap twenty-two feet for fun you know.

•

Curling

I forgot my lucky broom.

•

High Jump

I'm taller in the morning.

•

Boxing

He kept hitting me, so I bit his ear off.

•

Rowing

Sure we sank. But there was so much water out there.

•

Horse Racing
I stopped for the photo finish.

•

Diving

I banged my head on the board, and then I lost a kidney when I belly flopped, but I don't think anybody noticed.

•

American Wrestling

I guess I just shouldn't have lain on the floor for ten minutes rubbing my leg, waiting for the other guy to jump off the ropes.

•

Skiing

I didn't expect it to snow today.

•

Judo

He tried to trip me up. That's against the rules, isn't it?

•

Fencing

He lunged at me with his sword, so I had no choice but to shoot him.

•

Chess

Someone must have programmed that computer to beat me.

•

Cricket

I was put off when someone in the crowd sat up with interest.

•

Darts

I throw better when there's a tail wind.

•

Snooker

I forgot my lucky chalk.

•

Table Tennis

My opponent's shoes keep squeaking.

•

Tennis

I don't play my best game on grass. I'm more comfortable hitting a ball against the garage door.

ME, OFFICER?

Yet more car insurance claims

The pedestrian couldn't decide which direction to run, so I ran him over.

As I approached an intersection a sign suddenly appeared in a place where no stop sign had ever been before. I could not stop in time to avoid the accident.

I didn't think the speed limit applied after midnight.

I saw a slow-moving, sad-faced old gentleman as he bounced off the front of my car.

The telephone pole was approaching. I was attempting to swerve out of the way when I struck the front end.

I started to turn and it was at this point I noticed a camel and an elephant tethered at the verge. This distraction caused me to lose concentration and hit a bollard.

I was on my way to see an unconscious patient who had convulsions and was blocked by a tanker.

No witnesses would admit having seen the mishap until after it happened.

First car stopped suddenly, second car hit first car and a haggis ran into the rear of second car.

The car in front hit the pedestrian but he got up so I hit him again.

We had completed the turn and had just straightened the car when Miss X put her foot down hard and headed for the ladies' loo.

A PATHETIC EXCUSE FOR A CAT?

An American woman had missed a lot of work and her boss made her promise she would not be late, but on the first day back she woke to find her cat bleeding. The poor cat had a hole in its belly where an abscess had burst.

The vet was very accommodating and wrote her an official excuse, which hung on the boss's noticeboard for a *very* long time.

It read, 'Please excuse Miss X for being late in to work today. Her cat had a hole in it.'

LATE FOR WORK

First of all, define what you mean by late.

I lost the instructions for my alarm clock.

I got lost in thought. It was unfamiliar territory and I took an hour to find directions.

My car doors were frozen shut and I had to wait for the sun to thaw them out.

The car got stuck in reverse and I had to back all the way here.

I'm awake and dressed. What more do you want?

I was putting on my trousers and my head got stuck in the toilet.

My dog ate the car keys and I had to wait for him to take a dump to get them back.

I stopped to help an old lady across the road but she was really a man in drag. He pulled me into some bushes and beat the crap out of me. Then he said he was sorry and wouldn't stop crying and apologizing. So I took him for a coffee and tried to talk through some of his issues. It's good policy for employees to reach out to the community and help other fellow travellers on life's journey...rich tapestry...blah, blah, blah...

It was a really hot day, causing the molecules on the surface of the road to expand, with a significant resultant increase in the distance between my home and work.

I'm not late. I just thought I'd turn up early for tomorrow.

I overslept and dreamed that my job sucked, the pay was lousy and that you were an asshole.

It took me longer than usual to get the nipple clamps off.

I was looking up the word
gastroenteritis in the dictionary.

I have a morbid fear of making left
turns, so I had to drive to the end of the
motorway.

THE SPIRIT IS WILLING...

Missing work altogether

My wife was having sex and I wanted to
be there.

I was building a thermonuclear
detonator.

I was recovering from foot surgery:
yours in my arse.

I couldn't find a parking space, so I had
to turn around and drive all the way
home.

I won the lottery and now you work for
me. You're fired.

I had to change out of my superhero costume after a busy night of fighting crime and I couldn't find my civvies.

I won't be in today – my hair won't start.

I have a TV, a vibrator and pizza delivery. Why should I leave home?

I've found a better job. Serving fast food.

My head fell off. No, seriously! Don't you believe me? You want me to bring it in?

Don't give me your attitude. I have one of my own.

When I got up this morning, I washed down my Prozac with a litre of prune juice. Now I can't leave the toilet, but I feel good about it.

I was picking my nose and I pierced my nasal septum and just kind of kept on going. I think I scratched my brain.

I can't come to work today because I'm stalking my previous boss who fired me for not showing up. OK pal?

I thought this was my year off.

My wife's breasts are sore after her operation, so I have to stay home and massage them.

My husband's balls are really swollen after his vasectomy, so I have to stay home to keep them gently cupped.

The four-armed fisting monkey just escaped from the zoo. The police are advising everyone to stay indoors today.

I can't come to work today. I am too busy cutting the ears off my hostages.

My mother-in-law has come back as one of the living dead and I have to track her down and drive a stake through her heart. One day should nail it.

I have eye problems. I can't see myself coming into work today.

I have too many issues and I don't want them to affect my performance at work.

The voices told me to clean all the guns today.

My stigmata is acting up again.

I have twenty-four-hour projectile leprosy
… but I'll definitely be in tomorrow.

Constipation has made me a walking
time bomb.

I just found out that I was switched at
birth. It would be irresponsible and
illegal for me to come to work knowing
that my employee records now contain
false information...

My therapist is very pleased with my
progress. He says the hockey mask and
straitjacket are just temporary measures
and I'll have the report on your desk by
four o'clock.

I seem to have come down with
Attention Deficit Disorder and what about
that game last night so that if I cut along
the dotted lines and I still can't open the
tin I'll make sure you're the first to know
when I decide to switch to gas but thank
you for calling.

SLEEP? WORK?
SLEEP? WORK?

Caught snoozing at work

They warned me at the blood bank this might happen.

I'm taking a power nap. They recommended it on that time management course you sent me on.

If you paid me more, I might be able to stay awake.

I was working smarter not harder.

How can I work efficiently if you keep disturbing my sleep?

I was testing the keyboard for drool resistance.

This is in return for the six hours I lay awake last night worrying about work.

Damn it. If you hadn't interrupted me, I'd nearly worked out a solution to our biggest problem.

I love my work so much that I'm saving all of it for later.

I don't know what your problem is but I bet it's hard to pronounce.

I'm on a Stress Level Elimination Exercise Plan (SLEEP).

Someone must've put decaf in the wrong pot.

Boy, that cold medicine I took last night just won't wear off!

Ah, the unique and unpredictable circadian rhythms of the workaholic!

Wasn't sleeping. Was trying to pick up contact lens without hands.

… Amen.

STEEP LEARNING CURVE

Two cocky straight-A students missed an important Monday test after a weekend of wild partying.

They sloped into college on the Tuesday and were allowed to re-sit the test that afternoon after explaining to their professor that they had driven away for the weekend and got stranded after blowing a tyre.

That afternoon, they sat the test, in separate rooms, each smugly congratulating themselves for their cleverness. They opened the test paper and had no problems answering the first question, which was worth five marks. But when they turned the page they found just one other question, worth ninety-five marks.

The question was: 'Which tyre?'

FOR EVERY OCCASION...

Some big kids made me do it.

Sex isn't everything.

I was just following orders.

This has nothing to do with my mother.

At this time I am unable to process your order for the new CPU for your computer as our computers are down.

This is definitely a shortcut.

I could tell you, but then I'd have to kill you.

I have a high metabolism.

I was away that day.

Your Honour, I stabbed my wife in the back twenty-five times to hide her suicide from our son.

The cheque's in the post.

CRAP ADVICE

HOW TO USE THIS SECTION

There's an exception to every rule, except this one.

Some people say that you should take all the advice you can get. To this end, I've been collecting advice of every kind, from people in all walks of life – advice about work, one's children, escaping from wild animals, staying healthy, protecting one's home, top TV tips, and much more.

I now pass all this advice on to you. My suggestion – simply select the advice that is most relevant to your situation – then ignore it!

As someone once said, 'I may be gullible, but at least I have this magic fish...'

Want that promotion?
Need a pay rise?
Tried and tested advice for the
ambitious employee

Always remember...

All power corrupts. Absolute power is pretty cool, though.

If a thing is worth doing, wouldn't it have been done already?

Eagles may soar but weasels don't get sucked into jet engines.

The early bird gets the worm, but the second mouse gets the cheese.

The early bird gets the worm, but the early worm gets eaten.

Ambition is a lame excuse for not having enough sense to be lazy.

Hard work pays off in the future. Laziness pays off now.

Experience is something you don't get until just after you need it.

Doing a job right the first time gets the job done. Doing the job wrong 17 times gives you job security.

Anything worth doing is worth overdoing.

Avoid bickering and petty arguments by immediately punching anyone with whom you disagree.

Get behind early so you have plenty of time to catch up.

Never put off until tomorrow what you can avoid altogether.

When all else fails, lower your standards.

There are three kinds of people: those who can count and those who can't.

To err is human. To really screw things up you need a computer.

A picture may be worth a thousand words, but it uses up a thousand times more memory.

Never let a computer know you're in a hurry.

Give a man a fish and he will eat for a day. Teach him to use the Net and he won't bother you for weeks.

No problem is so big and complicated that it can't be ignored.

Laugh in the face of danger. Then run and hide until it goes away.

There are very few problems that cannot be solved by orders ending with 'or I'll shoot'.

The 50-50-90 rule: when you have a 50-50 chance of getting something right, there's a 90 per cent probability you'll get it wrong.

A pair of lucky dice can often compensate for a lack of good judgement.

If at first you don't succeed, call it a day and have a beer.

Don't use force; use a bigger hammer.

All work and no play makes Jack a dull boy who can retire at 40 and laugh at everyone else slogging away for the next twenty-five years.

IF AT FIRST YOU DON'T SUCCEED...

If you can smile when things go wrong, you already know who you're going to blame.

Before you criticize someone, walk a mile in their shoes. That way you're a mile away, and you have their shoes, too.

If you can stay calm, while all around you is chaos, you probably haven't completely understood the seriousness of the situation.

If you can't beat them, arrange to have them beaten.

If you can't laugh at yourself, make fun of others.

If at first you don't succeed, blame society.

When in doubt, mumble.

Don't be discouraged if you feel a failure. On some days even a hard-on can count as personal growth.

Practise random acts of intelligence and senseless acts of self-control.

Procrastinate now!

Assume full responsibility for your mistakes, except the ones that are someone else's fault.

Never compromise your principles, except to get laid or if there's a chance of a pay rise.

Stop judging others – even the inept and the laughable.

If at first you don't succeed, destroy all evidence that you tried.

AND NOW, SOME ADVICE FROM THE I.T. DEPARTMENT, WHICH YOU REALLY OUGHT TO PAY ATTENTION TO...

1. When you call us to have your computer moved, be sure to leave it buried under half a ton of postcards, baby pictures, stuffed animals, dried flowers, darts trophies and children's art. We don't have lives, and we find it deeply moving to catch a fleeting glimpse of yours.

2. Don't write anything down. Ever. We can play back the error messages from here.

3. When I.T. Support sends you an e-mail marked 'High importance', delete it at once. We're just testing.

4. When you call the help desk, state what you want, not what's keeping you from getting it. We don't need to know that you can't get into your mail because your computer won't power up at all.

5. When an I.T. person says he's coming right over, go for coffee. That way you won't be there when we need your password. It's nothing for us to remember 300 screen saver passwords.

6. When an I.T. person is eating lunch at his desk, walk right in and spill your guts right out. We exist only to serve.

7. Send urgent e-mail all in UPPERCASE. The mail server picks it up and flags it as a rush delivery.

8. When the photocopier doesn't work, call computer support. There's electronics in it.

9. When you're getting a 'No dial tone' message at home, call computer support. We can fix your telephone line from here.

10. When you have a dozen old computer screens to get rid of, call computer support. We're collectors.

11. When something's wrong with your home PC, dump it on an I.T. person's chair with no name, no phone number and no description of the problem. We love a puzzle.

12. When an I.T. person tells you that computer screens don't have cartridges in them, argue. We love a good argument.

13. When an I.T. person tells you that he'll be there shortly, reply in a scathing tone of voice, 'And just how many weeks do you mean by shortly?' That motivates us.

14. When the printer won't print, re-send the job at least 20 times. Print jobs frequently get sucked into black holes.

15. When the printer still won't print after 20 tries, send the job to all 68 printers in the company. One of them is bound to work.

16. Don't learn the proper name for anything technical. We know exactly what you mean by 'my thingy blew up'.

17. Don't use on-line help. On-line help is for wimps.

18. If the mouse cable keeps knocking down the framed picture of your dog, lift the computer and stuff the cable under it. Mouse cables were designed to have 25 lbs of computer sitting on top of them.

19. If the space bar on your keyboard doesn't work, blame it on the e-mail upgrade. Keyboards are actually very happy with half a pound of cake crumbs and nail clippings in them.

20. When you get a message saying 'Are you sure?' click on that 'Yes' button as fast as you can. Hell, if you weren't sure, you wouldn't be doing it, would you?

21. When you find an I.T. person on the phone with his bank, sit uninvited on the corner of his desk and stare at him until he hangs up. We don't have any money to speak of anyway.

22. Feel perfectly free to say things like, 'I don't know nothing about that computer crap'. We don't mind at all hearing our area of professional expertise referred to as crap.

23. When you need to change the toner cartridge in a printer, call I.T. Support. Changing a toner cartridge is an extremely complex task and manufacturers recommend that it be performed only by a professional engineer with a masters degree in nuclear physics.

24. When your computer won't power up, complain to us before you check to see whether you've switched on the monitor.

25. When you have a lock to pick on an old filing cabinet, call I.T. Support. We love to hack.

26. When something's the matter with your computer, ask your secretary to call the help desk. We enjoy the challenge of having to deal with a third party who doesn't know anything about the problem.

27. When you receive a 30MB (huge) movie file, send it to everyone as an e-mail attachment. We've got lots of disk space on that mail server.

28. Don't even think of breaking large print jobs down into smaller chunks. Somebody else might get a chance to squeeze a memo into the queue.

29. When an I.T. person gets in the lift pushing £60,000 worth of computer equipment on a trolley, ask in a very loud voice: 'Good grief, you take the elevator to go DOWN one floor?!' That's another one that cracks us up no end.

30. When you lose your car keys, send an e-mail to the entire company. People out in the Isle of Man office like to keep abreast of what's going on.

31. When you bump into an I.T. person in the supermarket on a Saturday, ask a computer question. We do weekends.

32. Don't bother to tell us when you move computers around on your own. Computer names are just a cosmetic feature.

33. When you bring your own personal home PC for repair at the office, leave the documentation at home. We'll find all the settings and drivers somewhere.

SAY A LITTLE PRAYER . . .

Grant me the grace to accept the things I cannot change,
The courage to change the things I cannot accept,
And the wisdom to forgive those I had to viciously
assault today because they got right in my face.

Help me to always give
100 per cent at work:
15 per cent on Monday,
25 per cent on Tuesday,
35 per cent on Wednesday,
20 per cent on Thursday,
and 5 per cent on Friday.

And help me always to disguise those
*   things*
that I left undone that I should have done
*   by 5 p.m.*

And let me not forget, when the world is
*   against me*
And everybody seems to be getting on my
*   tits,*
That it takes forty-two muscles to frown
And only four to raise my middle finger
and tell them where they can shove their
*   stinking job.*

WHY DOES IT ALWAYS SEEM TO BE YOU? PERHAPS IT'S NOT – AND IF IT'S NOT YOU, THEN IT MUST BE EVERYONE ELSE...

Hell *is* other people

In order to unravel the paradox that is mankind, we should examine the word itself: 'Mankind'. Interestingly, it consists of two separate words – 'mank' and 'ind'. What do these words mean? It's an enigma and so is mankind. 'Politics' also consists of two words, 'poly' meaning 'many' and 'ticks' as in 'tiny bloodsucking parasites'.

Never hit a man with glasses, use a baseball bat.

Learn to love the personality flaws of others – for some it's the only personality they have.

Help a man when he is in trouble and he will remember you the next time he is in trouble.

If you can keep your head when all around you are losing theirs, try landing your helicopter somewhere quieter.

Don't kick a man when he's down unless you're certain he won't get up.

A friend is someone who has the same enemies you have.

Make it idiot proof and someone will make a better idiot.

Dead men don't bite. But pretty soon they start to smell.

Half the people in the world are below average.

Be nice to the nerds and loners at school. You'll be working for them in the future.

Love your neighbours and love your enemies – they're probably one and the same.

When you go to court, your future is decided by twelve people who weren't clever enough to get out of jury service.

When you feel like killing someone, instead of doing something you'll regret later, here's a neat little trick to calm you down. Go over to the person's house and leave a pumpkin lantern on their doorstep with a big kitchen knife sticking in its head and a note saying 'You're next'. It will make you feel much better and no harm done.

...OR IS IT OTHER PEOPLE'S CHILDREN?

Advice for parents

A father is someone who carries pictures where his money used to be.

When your child wants to know where rain comes from, tell him that God is crying because of something he did.

Never raise your hands to your children.
It leaves your groin unprotected.

No matter how you try to protect your
kids, they will eventually get arrested
and end up in the local paper.

Children need encouragement. If your
child gets an answer right, tell him it
was a lucky guess. That way he
develops a good, lucky feeling.

To help your small children find you in
a public place, periodically fire a starting
pistol into the air.

When he's older, tell him he used to
have a brother, but he didn't obey.

The face of a child can say it all,
especially the mouth part of the face.

If he has a nightmare about monsters,
give him a gun and encourage him to
fire off a few rounds under his bed
whenever he gets scared.

Making your child eat gravel will
encourage a regular toothcare regime.

Explain that birds have to do this because they haven't got any teeth, so you'd better look after yours, etc.

Teach children the value of money by making sure they always know how much they are costing you.

Allow children to learn by making their own mistakes. Laughing at their stupidity also helps.

Children need plenty of space. So leave them at home alone at every opportunity.

Encourage independence by regularly losing them in the supermarket.

Children need to feel wanted. Each night, stagger pissed into their bedroom at 2 a.m. and wake them up to tell them you love them. Hug them tightly and start crying uncontrollably.

Children need to feel secure. So strap them down whenever possible.

Avoid pester power by using a little reverse psychology. Buy everything that they demand. The novelty of having every material need pandered to will soon wear off and when your kids grow up they'll give away all their possessions and go and work for UNICEF.

Avoid embarrassing them in front of their peers by forbidding them ever to bring friends home.

Foster problem-solving skills in young children by inventing imaginative scenarios to encourage them to think laterally. For example, pretend to have a heart attack on the kitchen floor and see whether they have the presence of mind to call for an ambulance. Be prepared to lie on the floor for several days, because sometimes children react in the funniest of ways.

Save up any food they don't eat and present it to them on their 21st birthday. As the truck arrives, explain that many people in this world are starving. Then tell them they can't leave home until they've eaten every last scrap.

ADVICE YOU WISH THEY HAD – OR HADN'T – TAKEN!

There'll be much more leg room in the back, President Kennedy.
ONE OF JFK'S AIDES

•

If you're ever in Alexandria, you should look up Cleopatra.
JULIUS CAESAR TO MARK ANTONY

•

You could do a lot worse than eat at Lucretia's.
CESARE BORGIA TO MICHELANGELO

•

Nobody's interested in your mother!
JOHN RUSKIN TO AMERICAN ARTIST J.A.M. WHISTLER

•

Moscow's lovely in winter.
MARSHAL NEY TO THE EMPEROR NAPOLEON

With the Italian army behind you, the war will be over by spring.
BENITO MUSSOLINI TO ADOLF HITLER

•

You'll never get anywhere in life sitting under that apple tree all day!
MRS NEWTON TO HER SON, ISAAC

•

Don't forget to check the oven!
HOUSEWIFE OF THE YEAR, EATHELBURGHA TO ALFRED THE GREAT

•

Stop hogging the bathroom and take a shower!
EUCLID TO FLATMATE ARCHIMEDES

•

Well, Mr Jack: fine gentleman like you, smart surgeon's bag – yer'll be more comfortable round at my place . . .
LONG LIZ STRIDE TO UNKNOWN GENTLEMAN

If you go down to the woods today, you probably won't see a soul.
THEODORE ROOSEVELT

WANT TO LIVE LONG AND PROSPER? DO YOU NEED THE BODY OF SOMEONE HALF YOUR AGE? PROVEN ADVICE FOR THE HEALTH CONSCIOUS

A healthy body...

Eat healthily, exercise daily, think positively, die anyway.

Gargle every day to see if your throat leaks.

Don't work out. No pain, no pain.

Learn from your parents' mistakes – use birth control.

Never play leap frog with a unicorn.

If your eyes hurt after you drink coffee, remove the spoon from the cup.

Don't sit on the sofa all day watching TV. Watch it in bed for a change.

If life gives you lemons, stick them down your shirt and make your boobs look bigger.

When jogging at night, be safe: shine a torch into the eyes of passing motorists to ensure you can be seen.

Give a man a fish and he will eat for a day. Teach him how to fish, and he will sit in a boat and drink beer all week.

Don't drink and drive. Do all your drinking before you get into the car.

Increase your life expectancy by living longer.

Live dangerously. Skate on the underside of the ice.

Save matches: chain smoke.

Weigh an empty coke can. Then open a new can and weigh it in between sips. Stop drinking when your can weighs the same as the empty can.

Obtain a wrinkle-free appearance by rapidly gaining a 100 lbs. That's if you don't mind the stretch marks.

A balanced diet is a cake in each hand.

To avoid the chore of slicing bread, buy bread that is already sliced.

Liven up dried spaghetti by boiling it in a pan of water before eating.

Red meat isn't bad for you. Furry grey meat is bad for you.

Always wait at least an hour after eating before you stick your tongue in an electrical socket.

One man's meat is another man's meat, after seventy-two hours of pioneering surgery.

He who visits the men's room with no shoes, returns with wet feet.

THREE THINGS TO DO WHEN YOU WAKE UP WITH A HANGOVER

1. Look in the mirror. Your face will be familiar, even if you can't remember the name.

2. Tell yourself you are simply experiencing the wrath of grapes.

3. Always listen to what your Rice Krispies are trying to tell you.

...AND A HEALTHY MIND...

Don't waste time reliving the past when you can spend it worrying about the future.

Smile in the face of adversity – and adversity will probably think you're taking the piss and beat the crap out of you.

Remember that it takes a big man to cry, but it takes a bigger man to laugh at that man.

Remember that no matter where you go, there you are.

It may be that your sole purpose in life is simply to serve as a warning to others.

Smile. It's the second-best thing you can do with your lips.

Honesty is the best policy, but insanity is a better defence.

Abandon the search for Truth – settle for a good fantasy.

Always yield to temptation, because it may not pass your way again.

Never go to bed mad, stay up and fight.

Don't let people drive you crazy when you know it's within walking distance.

Feel the fear and – stay under the sheets.

Nostalgia ain't what it used to be.

Always be sincere, even if you don't mean it.

It is easier to get forgiveness than permission.

Do unto others before they do unto you.

Laugh at your problems – imagine them happening to someone else.

If something was meant to be, it usually never happens.

The things that come to those who wait are the things those who got there first didn't want.

Don't do it if you can't keep it up.

Just because you're paranoid doesn't mean that they aren't after you.

Boycott shampoo! Demand the REAL poo!

Do not suffer in silence, if you can make others suffer with you.

Remember all of you is beautiful and valuable – even the ugly, stupid, and worthless bits.

Make a list of your faults today – then it will be easier to blame them all on your parents tomorrow.

Don't forget that depression is merely anger without enthusiasm.

Live every day as if it is your last. Eventually you'll be right.

HOW TO DEAL WITH LOVE AND SEX IN THE NOUGHTIES...

You cannot make someone love you. All you can do is stalk them and hope they panic and give in.

There is no remedy for sex but more sex.

Love your neighbour, but don't get caught.

The best way to a man's heart is to saw his chest open.

How to satisfy a woman

Adore, appreciate, beguile, captivate, caress, charm, cherish, coax, commit to, compliment, console, delight, embrace, empathize, enchant, enthral, hug, humour, idolize, indulge, massage, nuzzle, palpitate, pamper, phone, placate, promise, relish, respect, sacrifice for, savour, serenade, spoil, stroke, treasure, understand, venerate, worship.

How to satisfy a man

Show up naked.

USELESS WITH NUMBERS?
ALWAYS SHORT OF CASH?
SOME HANDY MATHS ADVICE

Find a penny and pick it up, and all day long you'll have a penny.

The quickest way to double your money is to fold it in half and put it back in your pocket.

A fool and his money are soon partying.

It is morally wrong to allow suckers to keep their money.

If money can't buy you love, rent it.

Save the lids from jam jars and milk bottle tops and use them as currency.

METRIC PROVERBS

Give a man 2.5 centimetres and he'll take 1.6 kilometres.

Put your best 0.3 of a metre forward.

A miss is as good as 1.6 kilometres.

28 grammes of prevention is worth 453 grammes of cure.

Spare the 5.03 metres and spoil the child.

AN ENGLISHMAN'S HOME IS HIS CASTLE – HOW TO LIVE LIKE A KING AND SOD THE REST OF YER!

Those who live in glass houses should change in the basement.

You can't have everything. Where would you put it?

A used washing-up liquid container with the top cut off makes a stylish cocktail umbrella stand.

Keep used oil from the chip pan for greasing long distance swimmers.

Save money on heating by covering your walls with tin foil.

Keep flies out of your lounge. Leave a bucket of horse manure in your kitchen.

Impress your neighbours by leaving broken white goods such as fridges and washing machines in your front garden. They will think you have just splashed out on a smart new kitchen.

Silence a dripping tap by sticking your fingers in your ears.

To stop ashtrays from smelling, encourage guests to flick ash on your carpet.

Pour 25 kgs of salt into your pond to prevent your prized collection of freshwater carp from freezing to death.

To prevent your toilet from smelling, urinate in the bath.

Place an old hub cap at the end of a sticky tape roll to make it easier to find.

To stop chairs from making dent marks on the floor, hang them from the ceiling using strong metal wire.

Cut a big hole in the top of your umbrella to stop it blowing away in the wind.

To prevent a small bag from slipping down your arm, paint a tennis ball the same colour as your outfit and attach it to the top of your shoulder.

Stop car locks from freezing by filling them with superglue.

Reduce condensation in your bathroom by only bathing in cold water.

A handsome book collection is often personal and difficult to replace. Copy each book and keep it somewhere safe.

Housewives: buy a Global Positioning System, an expensive hi-tech electronic device used by the army and even the SAS. Then when you are shopping, you'll know your exact position on the planet to within one metre of accuracy.

Remove the top five rungs from your ladder to make it safer.

To avoid hitting the wall at the back of your garage when driving your car in, place broken glass six feet in front. When you hear the sound of air escaping rapidly from your front tyres, you know it's time to stop.

Before packing away your Christmas tree decorations, smash one of the lights. Then next year you won't have to waste time figuring out which one isn't working.

Avoid lengthy supermarket queues by always choosing the till with the fewest people.

Take the guesswork out of remembering who you have lent stuff to by rubbing your belongings with a highly radioactive material (available at most municipal rubbish tips). Then use a Geiger counter to track down your belongings.

Avoid a dirty tide mark around the inside of your bath by always filling it until it overflows.

Let people know where you stand – wear the same socks for a month.

Don't throw away old toothbrushes. They are ideal for cleaning the corridors and decks of large military ships.

If the shoe fits, get another one just like it.

Always keep a full petrol can in your garage in case you run out on a long journey.

WHEN OTHERS WANT WHAT YOU HAVE: EIGHT WAYS TO KEEP IT SAFE

Buy a police car and park it in your drive.

•

Make your house look uninhabited. Board up the windows. Leave a burned out fridge on the lawn. Paint graffiti on the walls. Dig a tunnel to enable you to gain access to your house without having to use the front door. Then sit back and enjoy the lifestyle that you have worked so hard for.

Put a sign saying, 'I am a criminal' in your front window. A criminal will never steal from another criminal (except his mother).

•

Chain a vicious dog or poisonous snake to everything of value.

•

Nail a magpie to your front door. Burglars are notoriously superstitious.

•

Urinate (women) or ejaculate (men) on all your possessions. The police can then use DNA tracing to identify stolen property.

•

Hire a crane and suspend a huge glass dome above your house. Burglars will avoid a property with a conspicuous security device.

•

Pepper antipersonnel mines around your garden. However, this can be inconvenient if you have children or pets.

AS IT IS ON TV OR IN THE MOVIES SO IT IS IN LIFE. LEARNING FROM EXPERIENCE; OR, NEVER JUDGE A BOOK BY ITS MOVIE

If you crash your car it will always explode.

If you are a teenager, you will die horribly after having sex.

You must pick up your phone after the first ring or the other person will assume you are out and hang up.

If you are a woman who is running away from someone you will trip and fall.

Drivers: avoid being attacked by a *Tyrannosaurus rex* by keeping a glass of water on your dashboard. The sudden appearance of rhythmical ripples on the surface of the water will provide ample warning that a large dinosaur is approaching.

If you succeed in killing a monster, never check to see if it's really dead.

Never search the basement, especially during a power cut.

If you are in a high-speed car chase, you will always encounter the following obstacles: a blind man, a street vendor selling fruit, a one-way street, a pile of empty cardboard boxes, a wobbly old man on a bike carrying a string of onions and finally, a sign saying 'Bridge ahead incomplete'.

Move to New York as everyone can afford huge studio apartments, regardless of their income.

If you start dancing in the street, everyone else will know all the steps.

A car won't start trying to knock you off the road until immediately after you spot it in your rear-view mirror.

When they are alone, all foreigners prefer to speak English to one another.

At least one of a pair of identical twins is born evil.

Cars always skid around corners.

Bad guys always shoot worse than good guys.

Most laptop computers are powerful enough to override the communications system of any invading alien society.

It does not matter if you are heavily outnumbered in a fight involving martial arts – your enemies will wait patiently to attack you one by one by dancing around in a threatening manner until you have knocked out their predecessors.

When you turn out the light to go to bed, everything in your bedroom will still be clearly visible, just slightly bluish.

Should you decide to defuse a bomb, don't worry which wire to cut. You will always choose the right one.

If you are blonde and pretty, it is possible to become a world expert on nuclear fission at the age of 22.

Honest and hard-working policemen are traditionally gunned down three days before their retirement.

During all police investigations, it will be necessary to visit a strip club at least once.

All grocery shopping bags contain at least one stick of French bread.

All beds have special L-shaped cover sheets that reach up to the armpit level on a woman but only to waist level on the man lying beside her.

Anyone can land a plane providing there's someone in the control tower to talk you down.

Once applied, lipstick will never rub off – even while scuba diving.

You're very likely to survive any battle in any war unless you make the mistake of showing someone a picture of your sweetheart back home.

Should you wish to pass yourself off as a German or Russian officer, it will not be necessary to speak the language. A German or Russian accent will do.

The Eiffel Tower can be seen from any window in Paris.

A man will show no pain while taking the most ferocious beating but will wince when a woman tries to clean his wounds.

If staying in a haunted house, women should investigate any strange noises in their most revealing underwear.

Word processors never display a cursor on screen but will always say: Enter Password Now.

Even when driving down a perfectly straight road, it is necessary to turn the steering wheel vigorously from left to right every few moments.

All bombs are fitted with electronic timing devices with large red readouts so you know exactly when they're going to go off. (In the *Conglomerated Bombmakers Of The World Handbook*, page 7, paragraph 3: All bombs, made for public display and/or filming, shall have a LED/LCD readout for filming, theatrical suspense, and to make the actors look good.)

A detective can only solve a case once he has been suspended from duty.

Police departments give their officers personality tests to make sure they are deliberately assigned a partner who is their total opposite.

If you are being chased in a city, you can usually blend into a crowd of carnival revellers.

And finally: if you chant 'Jerry! Jerry! Jerry!' loud enough, the lesbian stripper always takes her top off.

THE FOUR LAWS OF CARTOONS

1. Anyone suspended in space will remain in space until made aware of their position.

2. Anyone passing through solid matter will leave a breach concomitant with their periphery.

3. A cat will take on the shape of its container.

4. Everything falls faster than an anvil.

NEVER OWNED A PET? COULDN'T AFFORD BARBARA WOODHOUSE? HERE'S HOW TO DEAL WITH ANIMALS

Never look a gift horse in the mouth. But do encourage it to crap on your roses.

●

A barking dog never bites. But it can still dump on your doorstep.

•

If you can't teach an old dog new tricks, you probably need to turn up the voltage.

•

If a pit bull humps your leg, you'd better fake an orgasm.

•

The hare is quicker than the tortoise, but the tortoise is uglier.

•

Save the whales.
Collect the whole set.

•

Don't count your chickens until they've crossed the road.

•

Birds of a feather flock together and crap on your car.

●

If after a disaster you have to leave town, take your pets with you. They are unlikely to survive on their own and can break the monotony when the tinned food runs out.

●

If you're a horse, and someone gets on you, and falls off, and then gets right back on you, buck him off straight away.

A FOOLPROOF METHOD FOR SCULPTING AN ELEPHANT

First, get a huge block of marble. Then, chip away everything that doesn't look like an elephant.

HOW TO ESCAPE ATTACKS FROM WILD ANIMALS (PROBABLY)

Attack from an unfriendly lion

Wait until the lion is five feet away and then ram a large pair of step ladders down its throat. If you cannot locate any step ladders in the jungle, then a small item of furniture such as a bedside table or a cocktail cabinet will do.

•

Charge by an enraged bull

Bulls have notoriously weak bladders, so make the sound of running water, or begin to urinate yourself, and the bull will stop dead to take a leak.

•

Crocodile attack

Look it straight in the eye, then stick out your tongue to touch the tip of your nose. A crocodile cannot stick out its tongue but it will be so impressed that it will try to copy you, causing its tongue to snap off. Then it will bleed to death.

Seized by a gorilla
Go very limp and start to make little
purring noises. The gorilla will think you
are a female gorilla. He will roll you
over and have rough sex with you after
which he will fall asleep, allowing you
to make his breakfast and then escape
unscathed.

•

Attack by a buzzard
Get a hobby! Buzzards are only attracted
to dead meat.

•

Swallowed by a killer whale
Motorways are routinely patrolled by
traffic police who will quickly come to
your aid. Do not attempt to escape from
the whale's stomach yourself as you
could become disorientated and stagger
into oncoming traffic. Use your mobile
phone if you are a woman on your own.

•

Attack by shoal of piranhas
Get out of the water, asshole.

•

Elephant stampede
Blend seamlessly into the herd by
putting your nose on your shoulder and
waving your arm in front of you. The
stampeding elephants will then run
around you.

•

Attack by a shark
Jam an oxygen cylinder into the shark's
mouth, then fire at it with your last
bullet.

•

Bear attack
Pretend to be a fish. The bear will bang
your head against a rock to stun you.
Then at least you won't feel anything
when it rips both your arms off.

LISTEN TO WHAT THE VOICES ARE TELLING YOU: ADVICE FOR DAILY LIVING

Gun control: use both hands.

Fool people into thinking you are enlightened by smiling enigmatically whenever anyone punches you in the face.

Avoid the inconvenience of getting dog muck on the bottom of your shoes by crawling everywhere on your hands and knees.

If you're sitting next to Elvis Presley on a bus and suddenly a large flat fish with orange spots and a leather jacket sits down on the other side, then you're between a rocker and a hard plaice.

Remember that a clear conscience is usually the sign of a weak memory.

When using a toilet on a busy train, avoid the embarrassment and irritation of strangers trying the door by leaving it open. That way everyone can see that you are taking a dump and that they should wait their turn.

If you must choose between two evils, pick the one you've never tried before.

Plan to be spontaneous tomorrow.

Light travels faster than sound. That's why some people appear bright until you hear them speak.

Conscience is what hurts when everything else feels so good.

If it ain't broke, fix it till it is.

Remember the nice thing about egotists is that they don't talk about other people.

It's frustrating when you know all the answers, but nobody bothers asking you the questions.

Avoid the embarrassment of tripping in public by repeating the same movement several times to make it look like a normal part of your behaviour.

The only substitute for good manners is fast reflexes.

Always remember you're unique, just like everyone else.

Avoid unsightly wear marks on the elbows of your favourite jacket by cutting them out and leaving them in your wardrobe.

Never underestimate the power of stupid people in large groups.

Fool your friends into thinking you are a member of the aristocracy by buying a large stately home in the country surrounded by four hundred acres of land.

Men are from Earth. Women are from Earth. Deal with it.

Go ahead and take risks. Just be sure that everything will turn out OK.

If you can't be kind, at least have the decency to be vague.

The easiest way to find something lost around the house is to buy a replacement.

If you think there is good in everybody, you haven't met everybody.

Living on Earth is expensive, but it does include a free trip around the Sun.

Find humour in every day – find
someone to laugh at.

Don't bother voting. If it could change
things, do you really think it would be
legal?

It's hard to make a comeback when you
haven't been anywhere.

Remember the only difference between
a rut and a grave is the depth.

Those who live by the sword get shot
by those who don't.

Just remember, if the world didn't suck,
we'd all fall off.

It's bad luck to walk under a bladder.

You can get more with a kind word and a gun, than just a kind word.

Opportunity knocks but once – and then shoots through the letterbox.

If you want to find Jesus, try to remember where you last saw him. But he's usually stuck down the side of the sofa.

The meek will inherit the Earth, after everyone else has finished with it.

Many people have fallen by the edge of the sword, but many more have gone over on their ankle.

If you're in a war, instead of throwing a hand grenade at the enemy, throw flowers. Maybe it will make them stop to consider how nonsensical and destructive war is. And while they are thinking, you can throw a real grenade at them.

All Michael O'Mara titles are available by post from:

Bookpost, P.O. Box 29, Douglas, Isle of Man IM99 1BQ

Credit cards accepted. Please telephone 01624 836000
Fax 01624 837033
Internet http://www.bookpost.co.uk

Free postage and packing in the UK.
Overseas customers allow £1 per book (paperbacks)
and £3 per book (hardbacks)

Other humour titles:

The World's Stupidest Laws – ISBN 1-85479-549-X
The World's Stupidest Signs – ISBN 1-85479-555-4
Outrageous Expressions – ISBN 1-85479-556-2
Totally Stupid Men – ISBN 1-85479-274-1
Stupid Men Quiz Book – ISBN 1-85479-693-3
Wicked Cockney Rhyming Slang – ISBN 1-85479-386-1
All Men Are Bastards – ISBN 1-85479-387-X
The Ultimate Book of Farting – ISBN 1-85479-596-1
The Complete Book of Farting – ISBN 1-85479-440-X
The History of Farting – ISBN 1-85479-754-9
Veni Vidi Vici: Over 450 Laughable Latin Phrases – ISBN 1-85479-441-8
Going to Hades is Easy – ISBN 1-85479-589-9
Witty, Wicked & Wise – ISBN 1-85479-593-7
The Ultimate Insult – ISBN 1-85479-288-1
The Little Englander's Handbook – ISBN 1-85479-553-8